GETTING TO KNOW THE WORLD'S GREATEST ARTISTS

P A U L
GAUGUIN

WRITTEN AND ILLUSTRATED BY MIKE VENEZIA

CONSULTANT MEG MOSS

CHILDRENS PRESS ®
CHICAGO

Dedicated to the Kids at St. Alexander School

Cover: *Fatata te Miti.* 1892. Oil on canvas, 26¾ x 36 inches.
Chester Dale Collection. National Gallery of Art, Washington, D.C.

Library of Congress Cataloging-in-Publication Data

Venezia, Mike.
    Paul Gauguin / written & illustrated by Mike Venezia.
        p.   cm. — (Getting to know the world's greatest
artists)
    Includes index.
    Summary: Briefly describes the life and work of the
nineteenth-century French artist known for his paintings
of the South Pacific.
    ISBN 0-516-02295-4
    1. Gauguin, Paul, 1848-1903—Juvenile literature.
2. Painters—France—Biography—Juvenile literature.
[1. Gauguin, Paul, 1848-1903. 2. Artists.
3. Painting, French. 4. Art appreciation.] I. Title.
II. Series.
ND563.G27V46   1992
759.4—dc20   91-35054
[B]   CIP
                                              AC

Self-Portrait with Hat. 1893. Oil on canvas,
18 $^1/_{10}$ x 14 $^9/_{10}$ inches. Musée d'Orsay, Paris. Art Resource, NY

Paul Gauguin was born in Paris,
France, in 1848. He led an
adventurous life, traveling all over
the world to find just the right place
to paint.

Old Women at Arles. 1888. Oil on canvas, 28 $^7/_{10}$ x 36 $^2/_{10}$ inches.
Mr. and Mrs. Lewis Larned Coburn Memorial Collection, 1934.391.

Paul Gauguin often used flat,
bright colors and simple outlined
shapes in his paintings.

Self-Portrait.
1889. Wood,
31¼ x 20¼ inches.
Chester Dale
Collection.
National
Gallery of Art,
Washington, D.C.

Sometimes he would use symbols from the Bible, like the snake, the halo, and the apples in the painting above. The symbols he used gave a look of mystery to his paintings.

Paul Gauguin is probably best known for his paintings of life on the faraway islands of the South Pacific. He loved the colors he found in the jungles, the native people who lived there, and their ancient customs.

Day of the Gods. 1894. Oil on canvas, 26 8/10 x 36 inches.
Helen Birch Bartlett Memorial Collection, 1926.198.

7

When Paul was very little, his parents decided to move from Paris, France, to Peru, a country in South America where Paul's mother had relatives.

Paul saw things there that he would never forget. Strange and beautiful plants, flowers, monkeys, and jungle birds were all over the place.

When Paul Gauguin was a teenager, he got to see other faraway parts of the world, too. First, he got a job on a cargo ship. Later, he joined the French navy. While he was a sailor, Paul learned how to box and how to duel with swords.

Paul's many travels and adventures may have helped give him the imagination he would later use when he became an artist.

Paul didn't decide to become an artist until he was all grown up. He had a family and an important job in Paris. Paul was a stockbroker. He made lots of money by showing people how to invest their savings wisely. Paul started painting as a hobby on Sunday afternoons with a friend he met at work. The picture on the right is one of the first paintings he did.

Landscape. 1873. Oil on canvas, 19 ⁹/₁₀ x 32 ¹/₁₀ inches.
Fitzwilliam Museum, Cambridge, England.

The Market Gardens of Vaugirard. 1879. Oil on canvas, 26 x 39½ inches.
Purchased 1953. Smith College Museum of Art, Northhampton, Massachusetts.

Many of Paul Gauguin's first paintings remind people of the work done by a group of artists known as the Impressionists.

Interior of the Artist's House. 1881. Oil on canvas, 51 $^3/_{10}$ x 63 $^9/_{10}$.
Photograph by Jacques Lathion, © Nasjonalgalleriet, Oslo, Norway.

Paul liked the soft colors the
Impressionists used and the natural,
everyday scenes they chose to paint.

Paul was able to meet many of the Impressionist artists and other artists who lived in Paris.

He learned important things about painting from them.

Artists such as Edgar Degas, Camille Pissarro, and Vincent van Gogh liked Gauguin's style of painting.

Some of the Impressionists even asked Gauguin to show his work alongside of theirs at an Impressionist exhibit. There were artists, though, including Claude Monet and Paul Cézanne, who didn't think much of Gauguin or his work.

Paul was encouraged by his artist friends. Soon painting became much more than just a hobby for him. It was practically all he could think about, even at work!

Finally, Paul Gauguin decided to quit his job and become a full-time artist. He didn't have much luck selling any of his paintings, though, and soon ran out of money. He moved his family from Paris to Copenhagen, Denmark, where they lived with his wife's family.

Paul's wife, Mette, wasn't happy about his decisions, but she loved Paul and knew how important painting was to him. She went along with his wishes for as long as she could.

Breton Girls Dancing, Pont Aven. 1888. Oil on canvas, 28¾ x 36½ inches.
Collection of Mr. and Mrs. Paul Mellon. National Gallery of Art, Washington, D.C.

Things didn't go well in
Copenhagen, and Paul decided to
return to Paris without Mette.

Paul Gauguin was always in search
of a place to paint where he could
really express his feelings. He soon

The Yellow Haystacks. 1889. Oil on canvas, 28¹⁵⁄₁₆ x 36⅜ inches.
© Photograph R.M.N. Musée d'Orsay, Paris.

became fed up with the busy, uncaring city of Paris. He thought there were too many rules people had to follow, especially rules about art. He found what he was looking for in Brittany, a part of western France.

It was there that Paul Gauguin's art really started to change.

Paul liked the unusual costumes worn by the people of Brittany and the beautiful countryside he found there. Paul started painting with brighter, flatter colors. He not only painted what he saw in Brittany, but added things from his imagination.

Paul's work soon became popular with many artists around Europe. They liked his new decorative style that was filled with expression.

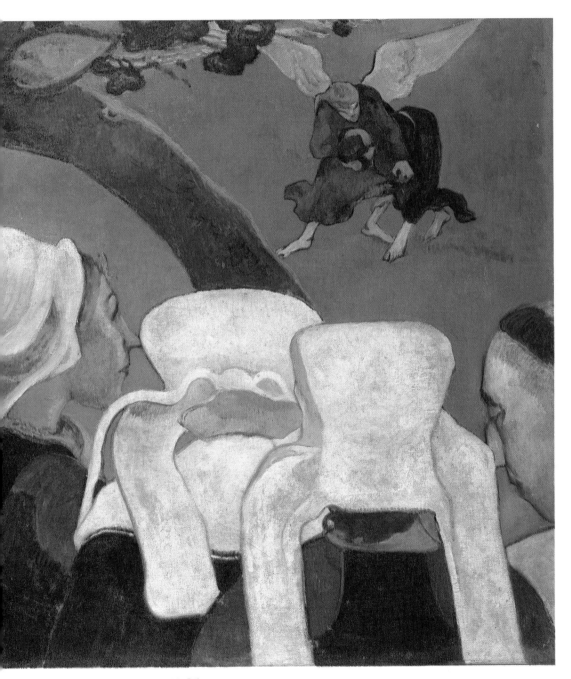

Vision After the Sermon. 1888. Oil on canvas,
28¼ x 36¼ inches. National Gallery of Scotland.

Even though Paul's paintings were well liked by his friends, he still didn't have much luck getting anyone else interested in them. He decided that to make his work better, he would have to leave France.

Paul left for the South Sea island of Tahiti in 1891. He told his wife and children that they would get back together someday. He believed they would, but they never did. Except for a short trip back to Paris, Paul spent the rest of his life in the South Seas.

Paul was a little disappointed when he arrived in Tahiti. It was run by the French government, and part of it reminded him of the place he had just left! Paul soon moved into the wilderness and explored other islands to find what he was looking for.

Tahitian Landscape. 1891. Oil on canvas, 26¾ x 36½ inches.
The Julius C. Eliel Memorial Fund. The Minneapolis Institute of Arts.

Paul worked very hard in Tahiti to
put his own special feelings into his
artwork.

Unlike the Impressionists, who
tried to paint nature as they saw it,

Fatata te Miti. 1892. Oil on canvas, 26¾ x 36 inches.
Chester Dale Collection. National Gallery of Art, Washington, D.C.

Paul Gauguin used his imagination to rearrange nature and create worlds that he dreamed about. He hoped that a person would look at one of his paintings and dream of their own imaginary worlds.

Where Do We Come From? What Are We? Where Are We Going? 1897. Oil on canvas, 54¾ x 147½ inches. Tompkins Collection. Courtesy, Museum of Fine Arts, Boston.

Paul was finally happy with the way his artwork was turning out. He was so excited about the painting above that he worked day and night for a whole month until it was finished.

The people in this painting seem to be wondering about the questions the title asks.

The beautiful colors Gauguin used and the way he made it feel filled with life make this one of his greatest paintings.

Even though Paul Gauguin was happy with his artwork, he led a very unhappy life in the South Sea Islands. He was sick most of the time, and very poor.

To create his own style, Paul often borrowed ideas for his paintings from Japanese prints, stained-glass windows, and Persian and Egyptian art.

He is also known for the wood carvings he made in Tahiti. Many of them have the same feeling the island people gave to their own mysterious carved wooden idols.

Right: *Pere Paillard*. 1892. Wood, 26¾ x 7⅛ x 8⅛ inches. Chester Dale Collection. National Gallery of Art, Washington, D.C.

Left: *Bonjour Monsieur Gauguin*. 1889. Oil on canvas, 44 ⁴/₁₀ x 36 ²/₁₀ inches. National Gallery, Prague, Czechoslovakia. Giraudon/Art Resource, NY

Paul Gauguin painted ideas that came from deep inside his mind. His paintings influence artists to this day.

**McLean County Unit #5
105 - Carlock**

It's fun to look closely at a real Paul Gauguin painting. You can see he often painted on cloth that was used to make sacks for carrying fruits and vegetables. He used the rough, bumpy surface to give his paintings a special look. The paintings in this book came from the museums listed below.

The Art Institute of Chicago, Chicago, Illinois

Fitzwilliam Museum, Cambridge, England

Kunstmuseum, Basel, Switzerland

The Minneapolis Institute of Arts, Minneapolis, Minnesota

Musée d'Orsay, Paris, France

Museu de Arte de São Paulo, Brazil

Museum of Fine Arts, Boston, Massachusetts

Nasjonalgalleriet, Oslo, Norway

National Gallery, Prague, Czechoslovakia

National Gallery of Art, Washington, D.C.

National Gallery of Scotland, Edinburgh, Scotland

Smith College of Art, Northampton, Massachusetts

Detail of *Ta Matete* on bottom of page 30.